Quirky scribbles

Sheena Hussain

BookLeaf Publishing

Presentation by *BookLeaf Publishing*

Web: www.bookleafpub.com

E-mail: info@bookleafpub.com

ISBN: 9789357691086

First edition 2022

Madre

Will the most heartfelt poetic rhymes ever be
enough,
Will the most genuine prayers ever match up,
What can we give back to her who creates,
How can we ever reciprocate,
What is ever as abundantly pure ,or as oddly
real,
What can ever be so ordinary, yet so surreal,
How can we ever give our Mothers the fair
amount of love,
How can we ever pay back to someone who
gave us us,
Every cell in my body is thankful for you,
Every day I'm grateful that I'm made of you.

Unmachine

Step out for a directionless walk.
Drive without maps on a Sunday morning.
Leave the highway, discover new routes.
Take a turn you have never taken.
Hop on public transport for a day.
Call people unscheduled.
Visit someone unannounced.
Have dessert before dinner.
Cook without a recipe.
Add unconventional ingredients.
Pick the next book randomly at the store. Play a
random tune and let the playlist continue without
jumping to your fav songs.

We are irrevocably machined to schedule our
meetings, our leisure time, our life.
Being in control is imperative and it feels
criminal to let go.
The world has us believing that not knowing
what's next is a sign of an unplanned
unorganized life.
Go ahead and disappoint the world.
Let the detour surprise you.
Let your impulses out once in a while.

There is freedom in not knowing.
There is peace in unburdening your mind of
decisions.

So go ahead! Leave the mundane rut.
Let the day unfold and navigate the amusement
that comes along
with not knowing.

Choices

Before you know it...
Random one time indulges become habits.
Habits become character.
Thoughts turn into your reality. Goals consume
your identity.
Words become stubborn opinions.A Facebook
comment turns into a lifetime of hate. An online
troll becomes a habitual bully.
Silence turns into distance. Solitude turns into
loneliness
A summer job turns into a career. A job turns
into survival.
An Acquaintance turns into family.Relatives
turns into strangers. A hello turns into an I do.
Friends turn into annual happy bday texts. Deep
bonds turn into passing thoughts.

Before you know it,
Life would have become what you chose this
next minute.

Choose wisely.

Dystopian

5

You drew lines and spread this fire
Named yourself saviour
Saved nothing but this hatred turning dire
With blood in your hands you see the core burn
now
With a vile heart you ensure the enmity grows
and how
But pages will turn, the dust will settle down
Your lies will unfold ,Your intentions will drown
There is godly power in voices which chime
together
Which sing songs about what's right
Which made us free from kings who trimmed
our feathers
Which brought the caps and robes alike
You will fail,
Your own blinded hands will pull your veil,

Someday, There will be another united fight
Someday, there will be another historical stroke
of midnight!

Covid and billions

When the dust settles

When the dust settles
Will it get better,
Will we be able to forget the helplessness of the
fading breaths that had to give up
When it settles, will it take down with it the
smoke from burning pyres,
Or the deafening cries from those separated from
their shared blood
Will the dust take down with it the unfairness of
this "system"
Or settle down with the selfishness which
emanates from this conscious oblivion

Where will this dust land ?
On the same space where the queues struggled
to get their turn,
To see their partners, children, makers be saved
?
Will the settled dust still reek of the chaos,
Of the mismanaged billions,
Of priorities that weren't really so,
Or of the sheer crime which is still unaccounted
for

Will the dust settle with a loud thud
Making our hearts race for what's next?
Making the mind numb, almost ready for a new
start?

Or will it dance slowly, swaying down,
Mocking the view it leaves behind,
those of names turned to grounded bodies
And masked goodbyes,
Some said quietly from far away

When the dust settles
It would have blinded us, cheated us of peace,
snatched parts of us
Cause you see, the dust is partially man made,
It won't settle
It will just come down, till it rises again

But in the moments it falls,
may we all be there
To witness, to register the remaining parts of us
And to remember what was taken and how
And stare deeply at those blowing at the fire
And get justice for those burning pyres

Make art not war

In appreciating times of benevolent sunshines or
in times of wet and greys
In expressing moments of hearts and love or in
those dreadful grieving days
In singing through a heartbreak or in dancing
through a fest
In simply admiring a picture or in actively
pursuing artful interest
In celebrating massive milestones or just a small
win reflection
In reminiscing about losses and failures and in
choosing life's next direction

We lean on art in different ways
We lean on art on all types of our days

When the world is a happy place, we share and
express and dance and recite ,
And when the world seems broken or divided,
please remember that art unites.

Live

Don't just exist.
Live.

Breathe a little heavier, feel the air calm you
down,
Don't just smile, beam and spread the cheer
around

Don't take those average steps, a little spring as
you walk
Let your words out magically, don't just talk

Don't just hum, sing so loud you lose your voice
Don't just dance, romance the floor and the
noise

Don't hide, no hesitation, what you feel you let
it show
Weep alone but not in silence, scream, let the
pain all flow

Love madly, disciplined hugs don't warm no
heart
Love with flaws, with passion and love as
beautifully as art

Wear the robe and the crown, who is to say you
don't rule
Be the master, be the servant, whatever you want
you be, you choose

Paint brightly the walls, the air, the soul, your
place
It's just once you have this gift, choose your
pulse and choose your pace

With each sunrise make the promise,

Feel a little more love, a little more cheer to give

You will smile more, you will laugh hysterically,
or just do a little dance,

But whatever you do
Don't just exist – Live!!!

Dear Empaths

Dear empaths
Give up
The heaviness of the worlds and heavens from
your shoulders
Shrug it off , you ain't Atlas and you shouldn't
be the bearer of weights of all kinds
Soaking in all issues inside your brain is nothing
but an effort in vain
Solutions won't come all from one head, why
then must you suffer the burden of the billion
morales dead
The falling price of human heads
The burden of struggling friends and
logger-headed family and an ever mooching
global conglomerate and political dead ends
alike
As though the success of everything earthy and
beyond resides with you
It doesn't
Stop claiming every feeling as your own cause
it's self destructive at it's best to be a
representative of all problems with answers
unknown
Dear empath

Re-think and be precious about the messiah-ing
and the social counselling and public availability
for problem
solving because in the end you are left with a
gazillion problems with no reciprocation but the
reeling of your own mind under self inflicted
stress and feeling
that you are owning these problems for a world
that's thankless
Thicken your skin and filter your brain and be
absolutely ruthless with what you shrug off
don't fear worldly disdain
Trust that the heavens won't fall as they reside
on every earthling and it's the collective
responsibility to keep it moving as it was meant
to be
and although change and peace start with you,
they won't be accomplished with you alone so
do your
bit
and be content cause
Dear empath
you are enough, and you are doing enough.

Unbecoming

Becoming
3/5/2021

Childhood and teenage impressionable naive
dreams created a picture of
how this future me would be,
becoming a someone,
someone,
always fitting, complying,
slowly morphing into a routined machine

And then
on a green mid April morning
this clarity hit
like an uninvited, untimely, slapping December
wind,
almost mockingly blowing on my face,
saying,
becoming who I want to be
is in expectation-shedding, in un-layering
un-aligning,
In realigning

that
rebelliously,

unapologetically,
becoming the truest Me,
is in actually unbecoming,

unbecoming everything the world consistently
said I should be
unbecoming everything else
to rightfully become the right me for me.

Friday feeling

In a world where you can be anything..

Be someone's Friday feeling, Someone's first snowflake on skin
Someone's first breath of mountain air, Someone's hair tie for their unmanageable beach hair
Someone's embarrassing peed-in-their-pants laughter fit , Someone's mindless moment when they just want to be a dimwit
Someone's "are you stupid" before a wrong decision, Someone's natural inebriation , Someone's ice cream on a summer vacation
Someone's warm tea when winter winds strike, Someone's comforter when they want to wrap and hide

Someone's diary for when their soul wants to spill , Someone's solitude when they just want some peace
Someone's pillion ride when they want to hit the road, Someone's "you are amazing" when the world makes them insecure
Someone's surprise check-in phone call when they are struggling silently

Someone's "who cares about the world"when
they doubt their abstract dreams
Someone's pearl of truth when the world is a lie,
Someone's humbling gravity when pride makes
them fly

Someone's first thought when they see a meme
or reel ,Someone's first thought when they
revisit an old phone gallery
Someone's first thought when a memory makes
them warm , Someone's first thought when they
hear an old song

In a world where you can be anyone, anything,
I hope you are an answer to someone, for
whatever it is they pray,
I hope you can help someone find what they
need, even when they don't say
I hope you can be someone's home, after a tiring
long day.

Love

Loving is not enough.
Bind them like a spell
Captivate them like a cloud
Warm them Like the sun itself
Find depths of seas in their souls and the
vastness of the sky in their eyes.

Loving is not enough.
Watch them like they belong in the louvre
Read their movements like poetry
Dive inside their mind to discover stories
Get drenched in their light cause loving is not
enough - you must look at them as they enchant
and bemuse

because

The trenches, the nooks, springs and winters,
there's so much to a soul
And loving is never enough
You have to embrace a world that's whole

Macushla

Macushla

I come for your soul like I go to the sea
Unadorned with layers, wearing but my skin
to dance with your waves, and sway with the
tides
to fully drown my weights
to carelessly float and unwind

I reach for your soul yearningly
embracing tight in highs and lows

Cause I find that in this exchange of chaos
is where our peace finds its flow
In this shared turmoil
is where our love learns to grow

दोस्त

बेकार की बातों में कई शामों को जिसके साथ हमने
गँवाया था
बिना सुर ताल जिसके साथ ना जाने कितने गानों को
यूँही ज़ोर ज़ोर से गाया था
स्कूल की किताबों से ज़्यादा ज्ञान जिसने हमें टिफ़िन
टाइम में सिखाया था
कॉलेज की डिग्री मिले उससे पहले ही जिसने अकारण
ही हौंसला बढ़ाया था
प्यार मोहब्बत की उलझनों से पहले हमदर्द जिसको
बनाया था
हर दिवाली और ईद में जिसको हमने अपनों के पहले
गले लगाया था
कभी पहाड़, कभी समुंदर और कभी यूँही छत पर घंटों
बातें कर, छोटे छोटे लम्हों को ज़िंदगी भर के लिए
यादगार बनाया था
हर ख़ुशी के पल और हर दुःख के मौक़ों पे जो बिन
बुलाए ही साथ चला आया था

एक दोस्त ही तो था जिसने दुनिया भर के रिश्तों को
एक दोस्ती के बहाने निभाया था!

शीना

I am

I am not..

I am not my job title
I am not my address
I am not my money
I am not my fancy dress
I am not my hair
I am not my face
I am not my colour
I am not my race
I am not my food
I am not my weight
I am not my exercise schedule
I am not my holiday dates

I am not..

I am not the parent I adore
I am not the child I bore
I am not the bonds I make
I am not the bonds I break
I am not my Facebook or Twitter
I am not my Instagram glitter
I am not my forwards or memes
I am not my stories or reels

I am..

I am a whole world inside me
And not the one thing you choose to see
I am more than a single piece
I am a small atom and the whole sea
I am made up of cracks and smooth lines alike

I have equal amount gloom and bright lights
I'm made up of emotions and of many variations
I'm a single day, the entire year, a lifetime of
creation

So stop, don't..

Don't make my parts my entirety
Don't single out the visuals, the materiality
Don't fix your gaze just on the ugly and pretty
Don't measure me all the time without my soul's
identity

Let's..

Let's have more meaning in what we want from
each other
Let's find more time for mind and soul matters
Let's focus on how we sit and make each other
laugh
Let's sit, and count the smiles and tears we can
craft
Let's focus on how we keep each other at peace

Let's only choose to remember how we make
each other feel.

Being human

Build the castle
Light up the wall with trophies
Display all the ribbons
Count your dollars and your stripes
Dwell all you want and
appreciate your journey

But when you touch another soul please just
keep all of that to be another human soul.

I admire your castle,
bow to your shiny medals,
I respect your stripes
and appreciate your progressive strides,

But when you attempt to touch my heart,
Please remember to skip your worldly
adornments
For all that we really need
Is for humans to be humans to one another,
Is for souls to be souls to one another
Is for hearts to be kind to one another

Meadows and poems

We should walk to the meadows
And sit by the stream
Merge with the towering green shadows
Soak in the mercurial beams
Untethered to reality
Perhaps talk deep with pages and poetry
Allow them to devour these mundanities

Let's go to the meadows and let's live through literature
Oh please, let's empower our poetic bouts to become our primal nature

Autumn

Fall is a very tricky month. I mean we feel extremely overjoyed just looking at colourful trees.

I'm not sure what is it about the trees shedding and changing colours that gets some really deep tunes out from the heart.
I mean of course it's an aesthetic heaven! It's like living inside a big beautiful bouquet, and the pop of colour is overpowering every time you step outside.

But there is definitely more than just the views.
It's that weird combination of various extremes.
It has the vibrancy of a kindergarten classroom,
the calming effect of cool breeze on your face after being out in the sun too long,
the embracing of that final goodbye, ones where there is a lot of love and cheer, the goodbyes you really put your soul into because you know you will meet again and say it again,
The bizarre excitement as well as anticipating feels about what's coming next and prepping for it,

It feels like that small morning moment you
peek outside and feel the cup of tea warm your
hands as you enjoy the view,
And that rustic retro feel which makes you
nostalgic not necessarily about someone or
something but you know in that moment that it's
a moment you will miss
It has the same colour as memories,
And somehow it makes you feel like something
is ending yet something new will begin and u
feel so much a part of it

Fascinations

Fascination with the air around,
  addiction to the imperfections and the chaos,

there is an inexplicable impatience that keeps
pushing from the gut,

 to look,
 to love,
to breathe in every single melody

and to breathe out every little melancholy!!